borrowed

COURAGE

bringing monumental women of the 19th century to life

REBECCA K. NOW

Borrowed Courage
Bringing monumental women of the 19th century to life
Rebecca K. Now

Published by Herstory Press, Saint Louis, Missouri
Copyright ©2024 Rebecca K. Now

Project Management: DavisCreativePublishing.com

Library of Congress Cataloging-in-Publication Data
Rebecca K. Now
Borrowed Courage: Bringing monumental women of the 19th century to life
ISBN: 979-8-9873049-2-1 (paperback) | 979-8-9873049-3-8 (ebook)
LCCN: 2024912625
Library of Congress subject headings:
    1. HIS058000   HISTORY / Women   2. BIO022000 BIOGRAPHY & AUTOBIOGRAPHY / Women
    3. SOC028000 SOCIAL SCIENCE / Women's Studies
2024

What People Are Saying...

What an amazing treat it was to hear from Elizabeth Cady Stanton, Sojourner Truth, and Susan B. Anthony! While I thoroughly enjoyed each woman's speech, I was surprised at how interesting it was for each one to answer, in character, questions from the audience. I truly felt transported back in time! — **Karen S. Hoffman, GatewaytoDreams.org**

That was an AMAZING program … thank you ALL so very much. I've had lots of feedback already on how great the session was and SO informative! Appreciate it SO much and definitely recommend! — **Amanda Kibbons, Erie Insurance**

As the most famous speeches of Elizabeth Cady Stanton, Sojourner Truth, and Susan B. Anthony are reenacted, we are transported back to a time when we (women) were not permitted to express our will in the political arena because we did not have the right to vote. The reenactors bring to life the struggle that eventually resulted in 19th Amendment to the Constitution in 1920. This performance along with the subsequent "in character" question/answer period should be presented in schools and public forums. It is both educational and emotionally moving. — **Kathleen Martin, Sisters-Christians Advocating Racial Equality**

I learned more about the women than I expected. It is a must-see for all women. — **Ly Syin Lobster, Founder of Ladies of Inspirational Success**

Invite us to join you for . . .

Women's History Programs

Diversity Equity and Inclusion (DEI) Programs

Women's Equality Day

Women's History Month

Black History Month

Now booking LIVE or Virtual Performances . . .

For more information, visit VoicesOfAmericanHERstory.com

Elizabeth Cady Stanton

Sojourner Truth

Susan B. Anthony

"The right is ours. The question now is: how shall we get possession of what rightfully belongs to us?"
—**Elizabeth Cady Stanton**

"We are assembled to protest against a form of government existing without the consent of the governed—to declare our right to be free as man is free, to be represented in the government which we are taxed to support, to have such disgraceful laws as give man the power to chastise and imprison his wife, to take the wages which she earns, the property which she inherits, and in case of separation, the children of her love."
—**Elizabeth Cady Stanton**

"Look at me! Look at my arm! I have ploughed and planted, and gathered into barns, and no man could head me! And ain't I a woman?"
—**Sojourner Truth**

"Be strong women! Blush not! Tremble not! I want you to keep a good faith and good courage. I am going round to lecture on human rights. I will shake every place I go to."
—**Sojourner Truth**

"It was we the people, not we the white male citizens, nor yet we the male citizens, but WE, the whole people who formed the union, and we formed it not to give the blessings of liberty, but to secure them."
—**Susan B. Anthony**

"We ask justice, we ask equality, we ask that all the civil and political rights that belong to citizens of the United States, be guaranteed to us and our daughters forever."
—**Susan B. Anthony**

Dedication

This book is dedicated to my mother, Phyllis—whose discontent with her prescribed role as a 1950s suburban housewife spurred me to look at women's role in society.
And to the future, I dedicate this book to my daughter Molly—may she and her children live in a more equal society.

Acknowledgements

I want to thank and appreciate my dear friends who've been a part of this journey with me: Caren Libby, Cynthia Correll, Cathy Babis, and Karen Hoffman. I could not have done this without your talents and encouragement. I appreciate Joe Taylor for evaluating my Toastmaster's speech in 2013 with the comment "All you need, Rebecca, is a costume!" Thank you to Allen Hoffman for providing me with an education from Webster University. I thank my dear sister Sue for reading all my blogs and essays over the years and coming to my performances and encouraging me. And for making me soup when I had too much to do. You are my rock. I thank my dear sisters, Marty and Joan, for their encouragement and support. My appreciation goes to Diane Droege for her editing and design skills. I thank all who donated to our crowd-funding project to help Voices of American HERstory widen our audience. And a huge thank you to Tia Adkins and Jenny Grace Morris for joining me on this adventure.

Table of Contents

Preface...page 9

Becoming Elizabeth.....................................page 11

Becoming a Trio ....page 16

Becoming Sojourner ....page 17

More Than a Famous Speech ....page 20

Becoming Susan ....page 21

A Woman of Purpose..................................page 26

July 4, 1876 - A Man's Centennial.............page 27

Why HERstory Matters...............................page 26

★ ★

Preface

Have you ever wished you could meet a person from history? Just reading about a historical figure, or anyone for that matter is not as fulfilling as having that person actually with you, answering your questions and engaging with you.

This book explores the journey of three 21st-century women, each of whom forged a bond and profound respect for a 19th-century American suffragist. It was the latter women's undeterred courage during the early women's rights movement that motivated this contemporary trio to embody their counterparts as reenactors, bringing their words, dress, and experiences to life for audiences.

We are three women who reenact Elizabeth Cady Stanton, Sojourner Truth, and Susan B. Anthony. We borrow courage from these monumental heroines every day and pay it forward as our audiences borrow that courage from us. We are passing the baton to the next generation, on the road to equality.

There are many fine books available about Stanton, Truth, and Anthony and we are not adding another biography to the library. Rather, this is a story of how we were called to embody these women and bring them to life. It is the difference between 'knowing about' our historical person and becoming our person.

The histories of these three women, recently immortalized in a bronze statue in New York City's Central Park, are not well known. It is in only the last 50 years that the study of women's history has expanded. Slowly, women's history, or as we like to call it, HERstory, is inching into public awareness.

So, what is it like to reenact, to embody, a person from history? It requires a deeper journey than playing a role with set lines, for when you fully embody a character, you open yourself up to questions after the performance. It is in that exchange with the audience that the magic of reenacting can be found. It forces us to go deeper in our studies, becoming subject matter experts on our character and the times in which they lived.

We hope you enjoy learning more about these extraordinary, courageous women in the pages ahead.

Rebecca
Now

★ ★ ★ ★ ★ ★ ★ ★

Elizabeth Cady Stanton

Becoming Elizabeth

I encountered, quite by accident, a woman who spoke up and made a difference in a time when American women were expected to be quiet and restrict themselves to a narrow sphere. There was no precedent for the powerful words she spoke, the wrongs she uncovered, the quality of her arguments, and the passion so evident in her soul. I was in awe of this outspoken woman from the moment I first stumbled upon her speech. I was incredulous to read the words that this woman used in 1848 and the demands she made. She was emphatic, strong, articulate, and made a convincing case for women's civil and political rights in 19th century America.

I was working on a public speaking assignment for my Toastmasters club and we were asked to find a speech from history and present it as an oral interpretation. When I accidentally came across Elizabeth Cady Stanton's speech, I knew it was fate. Stanton's speech, delivered at the first women's rights convention in 1848, launched the women's suffrage movement.

In this speech, she lays out the case of how women at that time were subjugated and considered less than full citizens in a republican government. They were legally obligated to give the property they may inherit, and their wages to their husbands. She had no right to child custody if divorce were to occur. A husband had a legal right to chastise, i.e., beat his wife.

When I performed her speech, it felt so right to me. My interpretation gave it a bombastic style, calling out the wrongs against women and the call for change. The evaluator at my Toastmasters club praised it and told me, "Rebecca, all you need is a costume." I was inspired.

During that time, I became an ambassador for a budding St. Louis nonprofit, Gateway to Dreams. The inspirational mentor of that group, Karen Hoffman, asked me to join a planning committee to help launch her new concept designed to help people realize their dreams. The group of twelve (mostly) women met weekly in a retail space in a declining shopping mall in Chesterfield, Missouri.

Part of the weekly routine was to go around the table and share our individual aspirations before moving on to discussion about the nonprofit launch. One day I shared with the group that I was really drawn to the speech by Cady Stanton and that I was thinking about having a costume made. The group was so encouraging! I was able to find a seamstress specializing in historical costumes and I debuted a public performance of the speech at Gateway to Dreams in February 2014.

I went on to perform at the Missouri History Museum during Women's

History Month in 2016 and later for women's clubs, historical societies, and the National Park Service.

I loved becoming Elizabeth and speaking her words. I later enhanced my costume, added a wig, and filmed my speech at a historic bed and breakfast in Webster Groves, Missouri using a Webster University student film crew.

Many women have never heard of Elizabeth Cady Stanton, at least in my age group. I was astonished that

I had never heard about this woman until later in my adult life. Why hadn't I learned about this in high school history class? Why had none of my friends in my generation heard of her? Those were the first of many questions that arose as I began my study of this woman, her century, and eventually the entire women's rights movement in this country. I started to question why the women's suffrage movement (getting the right to vote) was not a point of study in secondary schools. After all, this change affected the civil rights of half of the nation and yet it was barely touched on in high school textbooks of the '50s and '60s.

When I was working on my bachelor's degree from 2017-2021, majoring in women and gender studies, I would ask my classmates (who were a generation younger) about their high school memories. Did they remember how women's suffrage was covered in their history books? Their answers were diverse. Some textbooks included one written paragraph and/or possibly a photograph stating that women were "granted" the right to vote. There was little to no discussion of the 72-year struggle that preceded the passage of the 19th amendment to the U.S. Constitution, which legally guaranteed a woman's right to vote.

I became convinced that women should know about this woman and her lifetime of work, and that we all need to realize the degraded status of women in the 19th century. After I gave the speech, I was so curious about Elizabeth that I started getting books from the library and buying what I couldn't find there. I currently own 20 books by, and about Elizabeth. The more I learned, the more questions I had, and the deeper I became involved in the self-study of American women's history.

The Tale of Seneca Falls – The Making of a Precious Pearl

*"We hold these truths to be self-evident;
that all men and women are created equal;
that they are endowed by their Creator with
certain inalienable rights; that among these are
life, liberty, and the pursuit of happiness . . ."*

Thus spoke Elizabeth Cady Stanton at the first organized women's rights convention. This is the tale of how it began. It started with a complaint, an irritability of sorts. Very much, in fact like how a pearl begins its journey. Pearls are formed by an irritant invading an oyster's shell. The oyster exudes a substance to surround the irritation, and over time, layer by layer, a pearl is created.

The year was 1848. Five women—all homemakers and mothers— sat around a table having tea, and they started to complain. Have you ever sat around a table with your friends and complained about something? On this day, 32-year-old Elizabeth Cady Stanton of Seneca Falls, New York, was upset about her role as a housewife. While her husband was free to pursue his career and pleasures, she felt trapped. She was irritated about the status of women and their lack of legal rights.

Elizabeth grew up in a wealthy family, with servants and many luxuries. She received an excellent education, very unusual for a woman of her time. Her father was a lawyer, and as a child, Elizabeth loved to spend time in his office and law library. She remembers one incident vividly …

"A woman came into my father's law office, weeping. The woman's husband had died and the farm she owned with him passed on to the son who treated the woman most unkindly. Father told her there was no legal remedy. I realized the cruelty of the laws."

At the time, women could not inherit property so young Elizabeth decided to get a pair of scissors and cut those laws out of her father's statute books. Her father stopped her and explained that alone would not fix the problem. Perhaps the incident motivated her to find something that would!

By 1840, Elizabeth was married, had traveled to London, and enjoyed life in the stimulating atmosphere of Boston. Eight years later, she found herself in the not-so-stimulating small town of Seneca Falls. With three small children, housework, and her husband often away, Elizabeth was frustrated. And she complained about it at tea with her friends.

So, the women complained that day at tea, and this time, their irritation turned into action, They set an agenda and drafted a document of resolutions, using the Declaration of Independence as their model. They substituted "all men" for "King George" and titled it, "A Declaration of Rights and Sentiments." In it, they demanded property rights, education, employment, and equality under the law for women. Stanton and the women convinced the minister of Weslyan Methodist Chapel in Seneca Falls to let them use the church for the meeting and they arranged for a newspaper announcement. The next day, the Seneca County Courier published the call to convention to "discuss the social, civil, and religious condition and rights of women" on July 19-20.

Three hundred people showed up at the convention! Elizabeth spoke of women's oppression by the government and the patriarchal society of which they were a part. She went on to list 16 facts illustrating the extent of the oppression and insisted that women receive immediate admission to all the rights and privileges which belong to them as citizens of these United States. Elizabeth spoke of the changes needed in the laws, including the right for women to keep their own wages. Read the full text here: https//bit.ly/decofsentiments

Sitting in the audience that day was Charlotte Woodard, a 19-year-old girl who made gloves at home, as it was not proper for her to work outside of the home. Her father took all her wages. Woodard wrote in her diary about having her wages taken, "Every fiber of my being rebelled."

All of the women's resolutions passed unanimously, except the one calling for voting rights. However, when former slave Frederick Douglass presented an impassioned plea in defense of women's voting rights, the measure passed.

Elizabeth Cady Stanton and the convention were roundly criticized by the press. Many thought it was a sacrilege that the Declaration of Independence had been its model.

Seventy-two years later, in 1920, American women secured the constitutional right to vote. Charlotte Woodard, the young glove maker who attended that first women's rights convention, was legally able to vote at the age of ninety-one.

It takes a very long time to make a pearl. Just as it took a very long time, plenty of complaining over tea, and a lot of irritation to win the vote.

Our right to vote is a precious pearl, seventy-two years in formation.

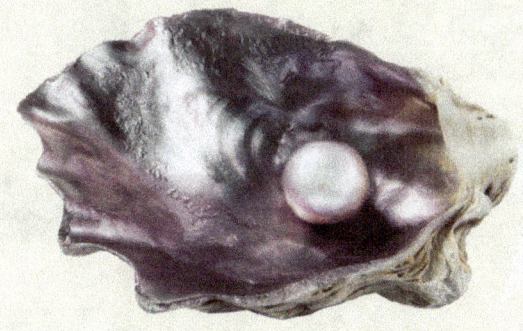

Becoming a Trio of Performers

After several years of solo performances as Elizabeth Cady Stanton, I longed to add more 19th-century women reenactors to the team.

Rather serendipitously, the perfect Sojourner Truth and Susan B. Anthony appeared in my life . . .

Tia Adkins

★ ★ ★ ★ ★ ★ ★

Sojourner Truth

Becoming Sojourner

Tia Adkins became familiar with Sojourner Truth when she was 16 years old. It was during Black History Month when she recited the speech, "Ain't I A Woman?" -the first time from memory. Then, later in life, she saw me performing as Elizabeth Cady Stanton and became became drawn to reenacting. What follows is my interview with Tia about her reenacting journey and how she personally borrowed courage from Sojourner Truth. ~RN

Rebecca Now: Who was Sojourner Truth in American history?

Tia Adkins: Sojourner Truth was an enslaved person, born Isabella Baumfree, around 1797 and she was able to work her way to freedom. When she was no longer enslaved, she went on to become an itinerant minister, abolitionist, and suffragist. She is most known for a speech that she gave at a women's rights convention in 1851. The speech has been since titled, "Ain't I A Woman." When I started to study her, I learned so many wonderful things about her. It really changed my view of her and of history.

Rebecca: What do you have in common with Sojourner?
Tia: Well, it just so happens that I am the age now that she was in 1851 so saying, "Ain't I A Woman" is much different at age 57 than it was when I was 16 and delivered the speech for the first time. I have been an independent woman, much like Sojourner. I am a minister. I like to use a little humor as she was known to do. Ultimately, she always stood up for herself, always. She didn't let anyone roll over her. As a matter of fact, she was one of the first women to sue in court for the right to get her child back when the child was sold into Southern chattel slavery, so she's the first black woman who also tried to sue. She was

from New York state and enslaved people were free there before they were freed nationwide, and they were able to enter into contracts. She entered into a contract with her former owner and he cheated her. Through the legal system, she was given some relief. She always stood up for herself, as I do, and that's one of the things that I share with her.

Rebecca: When Sojourner Truth gave that speech, it resonated and got into the history books. What was the significance of the "Ain't I a Woman" speech in that hall in Akron Ohio in 1851?
Tia: It's interesting that it was a woman's rights convention. I always assumed that the audience would have been women but the audience was mostly men, who were arguing that women did not deserve the right to vote. After she listened to several men make lame arguments about why women didn't need or deserve the right to vote, Sojourner finally said, "I'd like to say something about this…" and she began to counter each of their major arguments. Whether it was the men saying women weren't smart enough or women shouldn't vote because Christ wasn't a woman, Sojourner spoke with logic and humor and reasoned her way through all of their arguments. Just like Susan B. Anthony and Elizabeth Cady Stanton, she did not live long

enough to see women gain the right to vote, but she laid a really strong foundation. As the speech was reprinted in newspapers and became more popular, she became even more famous.

Rebecca: There's a bit of controversy over how it evolved in the history books could you talk about that?

Tia: The truth of the matter is there was only one reporter in the hall who took the time to transcribe Sojourner's speech in 1851, but it was not transcribed word for word. It wasn't a written speech. Sojourner couldn't read or write, she spoke extemporaneously. However, other people recorded the speech and at one point, feminist scholar Frances Gage added the phrase, "ain't I a woman" and sort of rearranged what was written in the paper and just made it flow a little bit better.

Rebecca: So, she functioned as her editor?

Tia: Yes, and it became well known with that edit, making it iconic. It became the famous speech that is often repeated. The word, "editor" is the perfect word for it because the gist of the speech is the same. I've compared the original with the edited version and the ideas never changed, it's just that that phrase was

added and frankly, it is rhythmic, and it is catchy. I think people remember things that are catchy. Therefore, Gage did Sojourner a service.

Compare the two versions of the speech here.www.thesojournertruthproject.com/ compare-the-speeches

Rebecca: How do you prepare to become Sojourner?

Tia: Putting on the costume makes a huge difference. It is so amazing to feel the limitations of that skirt and heavy petticoat, experiencing the way it slows your movement and restricts you that it really puts you in the mindset of the era. I mean women today, we don't even wear girdles anymore; we don't have that sense of restriction of movements. Just putting on a petticoat gets me

into the feeling place of being restricted and leads me to know what that feels like. In addition, of course, doing all the study that is required so that you can really appreciate the life of that person because when you're doing historical reenactment, one of the things that you realize is that after the speech, in a live performance, people can ask you about any aspect of that person's life. They don't have to limit themselves to the speech that you have given. I think that is one of the most exciting parts of performing is to answer questions and remain in character.

★ ★ ★ ★ ★ ★ ★ ★ ★ ★ ★

More Than a Famous Speech

Sojourner Truth was so much more than the famous "Aint I a Woman" speech she gave at a women's rights gathering in 1851. She was born Isabella Baumtree in New York in 1797, without a know birth date, as dates of birth were rarely recorded for slaves. Truth went on to meet with three presidents, including Abraham Lincoln. She spoke to congress and successfully won three lawsuits—the first black woman ever to do so.

Truth was an lifelong activist, a powerful speaker for the causes of abolition and women's rights, and was instrumental in helping freed slaves adjust to their new freedoms after the Civil War. She was "intersectional" before academics embraced this term.

Sojourner's life is a story of American exceptionalism. Born into slavery and sold three times in her youth, she remained a slave in the state of New York until she was 27 years old. Reflect on a person in your life who is in their twenties and imagine they have spent their entire life in hard labor, separated from their family, uneducated, and often beaten and terrorized. It is difficult to contemplate.

Sojourner grew up speaking Dutch in New York (New Amsterdam until the British took control and changed the name). Dutch slave holders thought it was good that their slaves only spoke Dutch so they could not communicate in the larger world of English-speaking settlers.

When she was sold to an English family, the mistress beat Sojourner/Isabella when she couldn't understand the English women's orders.

Sojourner/Isabella did grow to know and understand that she suffered from an intense oppression. Her commanding physical presence, great strength, and aptitude as a farm and household laborer provided her with a sort of resilience. In fact, her master forced her into a loveless marriage to insure he owned the prodigy of the marriage.

In her memoir, Truth recalls her mother telling her to trust in the stars and God. Isabella Baumtree had an epiphany when she was 43 years old. Following a calling from God, she renamed herself Sojourner Truth. How meaningful that must have been for a slave, so long "owned," to declare herself to be her "own" person.

After her epiphany, Sojourner began wandering. She attended abolitionist gatherings and was asked to give testimony on her life as a slave. She was a powerful speaker, moving audiences with her tales of beatings and the heartbreak of family separations. She convinced many audiences to support the abolitionist cause.

Sojourner never learned to read or write and depended on friends and family to read newspapers and letters to her. She would dictate her responses, as well as her memoir. Truth died in 1883 in Battle Creek, Michigan. There is now a statue of her in Akron, Ohio, in Sojourner Truth Legacy Plaza.

Jenny Grace Morris

Susan B. Anthony

Becoming Susan

Jenny Grace Morris and I shared a table at a women's networking event. I was wearing a name tag as Elizabeth Cady Stanton, so naturally I was asked about this. When Jenny mentioned that she had a background in theatre, I noticed the resemblance to Susan B. Anthony. After a few minutes of chatting, I popped the question, "Would you consider being my Susan B. Anthony?" It was a dream of mine to find the right reenactor from the 21st century to portray the Elizabeth Cady Stanton's dear friend from the 19th century! Jenny expressed interest so we agreed to meet for coffee. We talked more about the role requirements, she agreed to research Anthony, and the rest is history! (Or, should I say HERstory?) ~RN

Rebecca Now: Who was Susan B. Anthony in American history?

Jenny Grace Morris: She was one of many amazing women who dedicated her life to having people recognize that women were people. In the United States Constitution, it says "we the people" have a right to vote and that's funny that she would have to talk about the obvious.

I know it seems absurd when you look back, but that's how deep the culture of male privilege was. I know she was an abolitionist before she became involved in the women's rights movement and was involved in the temperance movement. She realized no laws were going to change, especially laws against women, unless they had the right to vote.

Statue in Seneca Falls, New York depicting
Elizabeth Cady Stanton and Susan B. Anthony meeting

Rebecca: Tell me about the speech you give as Susan.

Jenny Grace: Susan never saw the law as restricting her to vote. She saw it as it says I have a right to vote, and she went out and attempted to vote. Of course, the way the authorities thought was, "Oh no you don't have that right" and they arrested her. She thought, how absurd really to arrest her for doing what she had the right to do under the Constitution? So, she went out and she gave speeches all over her county where she had been arrested. Titled, "Are Women Citizens?," she explained the fact that "we the people" meant not just "we the men" but that everyone has this right to vote. Yet, the charges alleged that she didn't have that right? Why should women be deprived of their own wages and their children? Susan wanted to prove to everyone that the Constitution includes ALL people and that ALL are citizens.

Rebecca: How do you prepare to be your character?

Jenny Grace: As in any character, I look at the biography of the person, what people say about them, and ask what characteristics are like me or what characteristics I need to develop within myself. Susan was just such a passionate woman and I love that about her. She was tenacious - she never gave up. She was daring, she was courageous. These are qualities that I share but maybe not quite to the same degree as Susan. Oftentimes, I will see a word in her speech that resonates with me and I'll realize that maybe I haven't focused on it before. Perhaps I will do the speech with that word in mind and then incorporate it in other ways. Every time I deliver this 19th-century speech I want it to have relevance for women today. Here in our own country, there are women who are mistreated. I know them personally. And globally many women have no rights, so I always hope that not only the words, but the delivery will somehow make an impact that will influence our laws and our culture here in the United States and in other countries.

Susan and Elizabeth were close collaborative allies and dear friends. They worked together for 50 years.

★ ★ ★ ★ ★ ★ ★ ★ ★ ★ ★

A Woman of Purpose

"There have been others also just as true and devoted to the cause. I wish I could name everyone—but with such women consecrating their lives— failure is impossible."

Susan B. Anthony has the distinction of being the first American woman to have her portrait on a piece of US currency, the one-dollar coin, which was minted from 1979-1981, and again in 1999. This short-lived acknowledgment to this extraordinary woman is sometimes the only fact that some Americans know about Susan B. Anthony.

She came form a family of reformers and was always reform minded and purpose driven. She became a member of the Daughters of Temperance in 1846. Her life changed in 1851, when on the streets of Seneca Falls, New York, Amelia Bloomer introduced her to Elizabeth Cady Stanton. The two hit it off almost immediately. Elizabeth was known for her writing, speaking, and theoretical thinking. She was the American feminist philosopher of the 19th century.

To discuss either of these two great women by themselves is a disservice to readers, as they worked together for 50 years as friends and co-agitators for women's rights. Elizabeth's husband once said of their relationship, "Elizabeth forged the thunderbolts and Susan threw them."

Penny Coleman had it right when she included both women in one biography, *Elizabeth Cody Stanton and Susan B. Anthony, A Friendship that Changed the World.*

A singularly famous point in Susan's activism was in 1872 when she proclaimed that the 14th and 15th amendments to the Constitution included voting rights for women. With that, she voted in the presidential election that year. Two weeks later, she was arrested for "unlaw-fully voting." Before her trial, Susan traveled throughout Monroe County, New York, educating the public (and potential jurors) on why she had the right to vote. At the last minute, a change of venue for the trial was declared and she was tried in Ontario County.

Her trial was a disgraceful example of judicial malfeasance, as Susan was not allowed to speak in her own behalf and then the judge ordered the jury to find her guilty! She was fined $100 which she refused to pay, anticipating she could appeal to a higher court. Instead, of jailing her, she was released, thwarting the option to appeal.

Susan made a purposeful statement at the 1876 Centennial Celebration in Philadelphia, honoring the founding of the Unites States. Later in life, she criss-crossed the continent several times, supporting women's suffrage campaigns in the Western states. A reporter in Omaha, Nebraska observed Anthony at work during a convention and deemed her "not to be daunted by any obstacle."

By the age of 86, Susan was a beloved public figure, and at her birthday celebration that year, she expressed her gratitude to many at the festivities by saying, "There have been others also just as true and devoted to the cause. I wish I could name everyone—but with such women consecrating their lives—failure is impossible." These became her last words spoken in public, and "Failure is Impossible" became a rallying cry for generations of women that followed.

July 4th, 1976 – A Man's Centennial

It was a sweltering hot day, that July 4, 1876, as a young nation, the United States of America, celebrated its Centennial in Philadelphia, Pennsylvania. Susan B. Anthony strode to the speaking platform uninvited, as she was not on the official program. The National Women's Suffrage Association (NWSA) had requested a speaking role at the official celebration, but they were politely told the roster was filled. Instead, the NWSA was given five seats in the audience.

Later, after the official reading of the Declaration of Independence, Susan rose from her seat and approached the all-male delegation on the platform. She presented Vice President Thomas W. Ferry with the Declaration of Rights, a document demanding justice for women that she had thoughtfully written with Elizabeth Cady Stanton and Matilda Gage. As she left the platform, the audience eagerly snapped up additional copies of the declaration as it was being distributed by NWSA representatives.

The women then moved to the other side of the Independence Square and held their own rally, complete with singing and speeches. Gage diligently held an umbrella over Susan's head for hours to protect her from the broiling sun during the rally.

Susan's words that day still ring true . . .

"We ask justice, we ask equality,
we ask that all the civil and political rights
that belong to the citizens of the United States,
be guaranteed to us and our daughters forever."

Nearly 150 years have passed, and women still find themselves fighting for justice, equality, and the right to be in charge of their own bodies.

Why HERstory Matters

The look on the television interviewer's face said it all. Her mouth dropped, reflecting her incredulous reaction. I had just shared a few snippets about the status of women in the 19th century. During that period, American women could not own property, women had no right to their wages, and most colleges did not accept female students. In cases of divorce, men received complete and total custody of the children. And it was completely legal for a man to beat his wife for the entire 19th century, and well into the 20th century.

All this was a long time ago, when the status of women was comparable to that of a child, and her civil rights were sometimes compared to those of slaves. Astonishing, I know. Why would that matter now? Wasn't that two centuries ago?

It does matter.

Women fought long and hard to win the right to vote. Over 72 years and two generations hard! These activists were viciously lambasted by the media of the day, the printed newspapers. In her memoir, one of the founders of women's suffrage, Elizabeth Cady Stanton, describes the reaction of the press to the first Woman's Rights Convention of 1848 thusly: "All the journals from Maine to Texas seemed to strive with each other to see which could make our movement appear the most ridiculous."

Stanton, Susan B. Anthony, and other outspoken advocates for the cause made logical and clear arguments to improve women's rights for over 50 years. Their words fell on the deaf ears of all-male legislators. Former slave, Sojourner Truth traveled the country for years, speaking out for women's rights, the abolition of slavery, and the need to aid freed slaves after the Civil War.

These women were tenacious, resolute, and at times, disruptive. Their brave, unwavering activism defied the cultural norms of the time and the work they left behind is a gift. I think of it as an inheritance left to every woman in America by the women who came before. Are you able to attend a college or university and enter the profession of your choosing? When your parents pass away, are you able to share in the financial inheritance, or does it only go to the male offspring of the family? If you answered yes to either of these questions, thank the women of the 19th century who fought to ensure those rights.

We've all heard the cliché, "Those who don't learn from history are doomed to repeat it." We must first learn and understand where we came from so we can move forward in the right direction. To quote Gloria Steinem, "Women have always been an equal part of the past. They just haven't been a part of history."

Women played an enormous role in American history and deserve to be acknowledged. The voices of Stanton, Anthony, and Truth provide inspirational examples of courage, strength, and persistence. May we all borrow and build on those qualities by sharing their voices, emphatically and uncompromisingly. Why?

It Matters.

★ ★ ★ ★ ★ ★ ★ ★ ★ ★ ★

About Voices of American HERstory

Voices of American HERstory (VOAH) is an educational arts project created to engage and enlighten new audiences about women's rights history through performances, interactive discussion, and inspiring stories about women.

By using a multi-layered approach and making 19th-century events relevant today, VOAH offers schools in-person or virtual interactive learning experiences. Civic and community groups find that our performances, followed by a Q&A session with a performer serves as an excellent discussion starter for a meeting or corporate session on gender diversity. Available to all are professionally-produced videos of the now-famous speeches of Elizabeth Cady Stanton, Sojourner Truth, and Susan B. Anthony.

Each in their own way, these trailblazing women created a movement that resulted in the passage of the 19th Amendment to the Constitution, granting women the right to vote. They would not live to see their dream come to fruition, but their story and legacy will live on through Voices of American HERstory.

> More information, including how to support the VOAH initiative, can be found at VoicesofAmericanHERstory.com

About the Author

Rebecca K. Now is an author, innovative historian, and performer with a passion for women's rights history. Her latest project, Voices of American HERstory, allows her the opportunity to share the legacies of often overlooked women suffragists as well as shine a light on contemporary women making history. She enjoys portraying 19th-century feminist philosopher, Elizabeth Cady Stanton for various audiences.

Rebecca came of age in the 20th century during the women's liberation movement and claims affinity to all three waves of feminism, often joking that she "breathes in three centuries."